There is Room in a Horse for the Whole Boy

Poems

Barbara Saunier

ISBN: 9781968226039

Grand River Poetry Press
Grand Rapids, Michigan

This collection is dedicated to my dad, who 'got' me.

For the poet, among the most difficult experiences to explore and create is the paradoxical fusion of the opposing, contradicting, disruptive feelings we wake to every morning. And yet Saunier also affirms that we must wake each day and humanely walk into the the staggering experience of being human. In her unpretentious sonnet "Goose Down" Saunier blends wonder, shock, grief, joy, mystery.... They cannot be separated. All Saunier's perceptive poems evoke and embody the constancy of our contradictory inner experience. But to be confronted by these courageous poems is in the end to be strengthened.

—Jack Ridl, author of *All At Once*, *Losing Season*, and *Practicing to Walk Like a Heron*

[Using] form, language, and humor, Barbara Saunier puts us right into...rural living. These poems hold no secrets, instead they offer stunning revelations of life, death, the bovine cry for her calf, the opossum that needs killing. This is a book that honors the callused hand, the whole of the horse,...the laundered bed sheets, toasted cheese sandwiches, and the barn swallow's "rookie mistake" leaving it dead but "no less worthy," in this poet's imagination, than "fine porcelain."

—Joy Gaines-Friedler, author of *Secular Audacity* and *Capture Theory*

"The sense of tone and place in this collection [is] strong and distinct. The stark sense of longing mixed with the specific details work well to captivate the reader. Each poem presents beautifully written imagery that represents a deep connection with the natural world.... Readers highlighted the poems "Of Which Little Boys are Made" and "Carry Me" for their uniqueness. Both pieces do a magnificent job of illustrating the level of craft in which Barbara Saunier operates. "Goose Down" gave us a touching moment that highlighted the beauty that can be found in death and the circle of life."

—*Summit Series of CMICH Press*

With an almost heady immersion into the granular details of the world around her, Barbara Saunier brings her whole heart to natural processes and finds beauty and transformation in our "living soil." From meditations on the carcass of a barn swallow "worthy of...wrought gold," a weasel "genie" on ice among the frozen peas, and the heart-rending rendering of a horse into the glue that will enable the voice of the violin, the poems in *There Is Room in a Horse for the Whole Boy* extract "sacraments of decay" and richly rewarding song.

—Terry Bohnhorst Blackhawk, author of *One Less River* and *Maumee, Maumee*

Hide & Seek

Fences

Choir

Sanctuary

There is Room in a Horse For the Whole Boy

The sanctuary of her vaulted ribs
receives a boy at hide and seek
like the cupboard under the kitchen sink —
a foreign place, yet free from his fears
of the secure hand lost and as close
as the call to lunch — a place as common
and as mythic as the womb.

The travel side, too, of a horse
grants a boy full-bodied mercy. He lies
astride along the long back of her,
his four limbs in a play of joints draped
down her planes of muscle overlying bone.
When her solid skin bucks at flies,
his own ribs like knuckles
seek to knit with hers. The shared space of their lungs
rises and falls, and in the choir of his belly a heart
bigger than his own cage of ribs
echoes the business of their good blood.

And where is there asylum for the whole horse
if not in a boy who smolders with the heat
of summer grass, whose chapel rings with movement?
As one, they bow to the stone against the sole
and to the weight of rain on their backs. Their one flesh
can tell fear from nurture, salt from sweet,
itch from scratch. As one flesh they know
the space taken up by fences.

Hide & Seek

Argiope, Goddess of Small Repute

If I were a goddess of even small repute,
I would take my cues from Argiope,
spider of garden and fencerow.
I would not scuttle away
like some brown recluse
from the lover who spurned me. I'd
paint my face silver! wear robes of ebony
and gold, throw the drapes open wide, slay
snapping turtles for soup —
                        And if I got rousted
by things unseen or seen, you would not
catch me admitting doubt.
                       Still, of extravagant
quiet, of old dramas writ small, Argiope
makes room on the flesh of her back
for yellow sun and black earth to settle
their differences. Between yarrow and golden rod,
she paces off coordinates on x and y, in her spiral
writes a gospel of rivet and weld.
When the vowels of summer plainsong
lean into her web — *Dominus Exsultemus,*
In Paradisum angeli — they bow
but do not break it. Her eight legs comb
the space between tones, they groom
the counsel that keeps her. And when
some errant grasshopper thrills her web with banjo twang,
she restores all stillness with a bite.
      She of extravagant reach
      is no less chaste than a circle in a square —

                If
I were a goddess of even small repute
I'd do well to take cues from Argiope:
Travel light, mind where I step,
make a new web tomorrow

from the web I eat today. And before
I forgive me my trespasses,
        measure twice.

Gaia, Mother Goddess of Life and the Bountiful Earth, Consecrates the Bones

She suspects below ground they've been
eavesdropping
— ear to the main chance, listening
to her cycles of frost and thaw, crack

and susurration. Now the bones
have nudged themselves into reverse,
escaping the dark clutch of worms and
come shyly into her hand

for metamorphosis into their next life. Gaia
grants an ancient precedent:
shoulder blades lashed into hoes, fish hooks
ground from ribs and toes, bone needles allemanding

left and right through flaps of pliant hide — even bones
thrown in divination. She holds them up:
these vertebrae she might string like beads to ornament
her waist, her wrists, her throat. Or to enumerate

the stars. She could make of this long bone
a whistle — pipe into song the breath
that's left it —
       But her own bones want

a precedent older still: the marrow of their story told
as only she can tell it. From the chalice of her own skull
Gaia sips the birth and death and birth
of common tribute, hears the sough

of common cause. A living soil
wants leavening — frost and thaw and flesh
and bone.   Leave it.
       Leave it.

Revelation, or
God Justifies the Carnivorous Cobra Lily
to Winged and Creeping Things

By all means, if you're thirsty,
    come. Flank
        the cobra lily's forked
            tongue and navigate her narrow green
            way toward nectar. Come
        like an old man propping up
    his way with a cane, the mother
shepherding her brood, hands
active as antennae — like the somber
        child coming forth at First Communion
            expecting to be saved.   Mind you,
          sawfly, marshfly, beetle, punkie: What's
    honey to the mouth may be bitter
to the stomach. Still, let's
    let your example show others
        the way. You come.

                How it works
                    is that light from above
            flushes out misgiving, the lily's narthex
                domed in windows
            stained with a sun that would
        guide an insect up
    and out and on its way again.

I say *would*. You see, the genius of cobra lily
    is that her luster
    isn't halo, torch, or lamp
        for all its light; nor glass
        nor some migrating current in a glass
            sea. It's a fun house of false
                exits, a serpent's guile. Even
            as the lily's dome recedes, her throat
        directs you in and down until you stagger. I ask you,
            Why wrestle?

Make yourself ready
like a bride. In cobra lily's belly,
it's not fire will consume your flesh
but juices, a few bacteria. Yours
and the flesh of kings and captains, others
of your kind. Never mind. Take
the water, drink deep. Digestion
is another word for Alpha and Omega,
decay for everlasting life. Amen. Everlasting,
even to a thousand years.

Wingbound IV: Dénouement

Pencil feet scribble your story
from inside the long, hollow bone
of the downspout, a grammar
unfamiliar to starlings.
Next to the nibs of your toes
your bird lips move without voice:
No call would remember you to the flock
anyway — that cursive exclamation.

Only one star hangs above
your dark flyway — complication enough
but horizon still to navigate by
were your hollow-boned limbs able to compose
a long, narrow chapter of lift. As it is

your migration toward gravel
takes seasons of heat and cold,
heat and wet and cold. Your lodestar
flickers out. When finally you emerge
clumsy in a downpour, you're little more
than a diary of small bones
and the few faded feathers
caressing your skull. The whorling flock
writes its flight over your sketchy notes,
refuting your broken leg,
your parchment keel: their wings
a comedy of conjugation; your wings
a farce, and twisted wrong-side up.

Weasel On Ice

I guess the genie is out of the bottle.
And yet who knew it even *was* a genie?
that wisp of an idea that stands
for the best and the most and the least and makes us see
what isn't there.
                A genie!
and here she thought it was only
a weasel — dead
on the barn floor. Not so much as a smudge
in its fur. No cat
was taking credit.
She'd never seen a weasel before — a wonder
in russet and ivory on a barn floor
otherwise spare of wonder.

How could she not pick it up? It just fit
her hand. With her finger
she traced its jaw and feathered
its toes. Sought a heartbeat
in vain. William Stafford might have flipped it
onto the manure spreader, and who
would fault him? But she
slipped it, pagan spirit and all, into a baggie —

Though the barn and floor yet stand and
different cats leave their remnants of kill
— wonders in smear and feather —
she has not seen a weasel
since. Chipmunk, vole, muskrat, yes, but
in these twenty years, no weasel — save
the russet ivory genie tucked behind the frozen peas,
become now a secret handshake
between us.

The Kissing Post

After the school bus flashes her red to the curb,
her mother's list tells her start supper, run a load
of laundry. Upstairs water heats for potatoes,
while in the basement darks and lights collapse
into piles of cotton and permanent press. She is

already fifteen. If basketball and baby sitting scuff
the polish off her bitten nails, thoughts of her poster boy
husk her — he of the cocked shoulder and the fixed
gaze, who speaks her name during study hall
so only she hears.

As the washtub fills, a load-bearing post
beckons from the dance floor. What it lacks
of her bed pillow's *you baby*, it stirs
with the *hello there* of height and something
pelvic. Her chambray eyes close.

While the clothes take on water, one hand traces
the dimpled knot at the nape of the clothesline
and the fingers of her other hand tease
the pull chain of the bare light bulb,
tugging some privacy

on. Shirts and slacks tangle
in a figment of breasts and thighs.
The lift of her chin beguiles her *yeah-*
yeah to the exploration of hip, the post's
ingrained memory of *lookin' good.*

How the agitator in the washtub chafes those seams
when her suitor leans to scoop her close,
and steam from the boil upstairs rattles the pot lid.
Their breath rises, and lips part barely.
                                              Her fingernails
grow tapered and long.

Touch My Face

Smuggle it in if you have to
— past this homemade cotton mask
of recommended double layers,
that threatens you'll mistake me
for a sock puppet. Almost any
touch will do. Effervescence,
or a straggle of spider web,
a dusting of pollen
from dandelion. A dusting
of dust from dust.
Perhaps your breath — a touch
dispersed, like seed,
by wind. Touch my face
with terrycloth soaked
in cool water.

Maybe I will shuck the mask
and let my fingers trespass
over my own eyes and lips — fingers
haunted by concern, by puzzlement.
By a certain
prospect. My fingers
— or yours.

Touch my face so its contours
breach the contours
of your shoulder and
your neck, and touch my face
with a touch I won't mistake
for rain or tears
or sweat that creeps
from my hairline down
over my cheek and chin
— for the tremor of light pious
off the wings of honeybees.

*

Touch my face with a touch I won't mistake
for the bamboo chime hanging
under the eave
or the distant barking of dogs.

Goose Down

A Canada goose down in the pasture
has died with his head under his wing.
A nickel's worth of last night's rain
bejewels that wing, the perfect curve

of a wrist. Like chick to egg, his parts
conform. The terrier puts her nose to the wing
and finds it too still for sport, too fresh
for the sacraments of decay. The red mare

cannot find a place for her fear; he could be
puma, tarp, umbrella. She scatters her fear
to the fencerows. Me, I sit in the grass
and draw the goose over my lap, a feather

counterpane. I stroke him, kindred soul
in the heat we've had in common. He tells me
of the comforts of my own company, that
it is not so bad to die alone,
head tucked under a wing.

Of Which Little Boys Are Made

Grandfather lines them up on the picnic table —
fat puppies with muddy voices.
In the yard while the terrier sports a laughing boy
from her end of a knotted towel,
he strops the knife blade on his thigh
and rocks it through the first sprig of a tail
that already could speak for itself. The pup's shriek
boils the terrier boyless, she spews
her voice over them. Four puppies and the boy, too,
shriek with a fear of falling, of swaddling
laid open and a nest riven. They dizzy the bitch
incandescent with bay, with tongue — their cries
elemental as salt. And Grandfather
scuds the pupless tails into the boy's shirt pocket.
"Take 'em to school," the old man says.
"Show 'em off."

Four tails silenced of their small black exclamations,
— their white-tipped points having nothing left to say
now shy the weight of their wags.

Give a Man a Fish

Whether he will eat for only today
or for his whole life through, the figure tucked
inside a carapace of Carhartts the next hole over
shoals the fish the bayou gives him
on the ice around his feet. Cold blood
will stir their gills again in time to meet
his knife. But for me, feeding

is little cause to fish. The thin shawl
of the sun, the dark glove of mulch
that warms the worm when all other earth
is seized numb — I come
for the humility, to void the house where even
carpet lies. To accept the cleansing arc
of horizon in the hole's five-inch rim.

I ruche another worm onto the hook. In spite of me,
each tug on the line ticks desire. No doubt
the crows overhead would puzzle over
my technique. Submerged pilings rankle
the barb. — Maybe my son swims
among the bluegill and the warmouth bass:
I will know him if he ever takes the bait.

I throw back the fish, keep the worm —
in spite of me, try again. If not my son in there,
my own lost skin. It must be somewhere —
mink, heron, painted turtle. I will know I'm getting close
when I catch that first fish with my teeth.

Carry Me

…but now and then, from
time to time, if you would just

carry me, prop me up, steady me — Let me
lean on you, I ask, just till the boom
stops lurching. I don't mean

like the tabby cat carries the vole, slack
from the pounce of feline sport, or
like the back of the envelope carries

a grocery list. More, I hope, like
the pond in the pasture carries the visiting
geese, carries reflections of the mare,

the white oak — all on glassy shoulders, without
burden. Sometimes a good strong wind
carries a rose cone stumbling

over fields from someone's yard to lodge
against the thornapple. But think how April
carries the tadpole to the surface of ditchwater

— for a sip of air and out of sight again
where surely it can still see
what needs seeing. . . . Like that — if you can,

please, and would. Even as cattails carry
their heads — each as much the one
as the other. As the fallow edge of the cornfield

carries the hoof print of the doe, and the greensward
a buck's shed antler — which I then carry home,
a gift for you.

Navigating Toward the Foothills of November

Above the big lake flocks of winter clouds gather
for their descent to fenced pastures. The low sun sears
the wool of their underbellies, scudding them along.
Below, the farm house tucks in behind the barn.
The wind bucks. Her chin seeks refuge
in the collar of her sweater.

Navigating toward the foothills of November
she paces off the migration of hours
that will place a stone over the month of your death.
Her finger maps the serpentine route of days
that reach back over the plains of a leafy middle age
to your last unharvested summer.

In her kitchen, outcroppings of potato and lean meat
breach the stew. What she doesn't eat tonight
she will freeze for later. Wind outside her window
mounts leaves across the sleet that scumbles
distant summits. It drives them up the gills and through
the basins of your familiar gestures. At the shore,
sand singes your windspent voice.

Wind drives the mice indoors. They range overhead
and between drawers, in the walls dribble shavings
to help them find their way back. Rose hips and
the dog's kibble collect in unlikely places.
The gate in the yard bangs closed and open
for her climb into the loose terrain
of your unfamiliar absence.

—for WFD

Gaia, Mother Goddess of Life and the Bountiful Earth, Wonders at Spiritus Rerum

Spell-eyed. A misgiving in the grass. She
finds him just about where lightning
grilled that cow and left her calf standing
vexed and stupid. As though now there might be
static in the pith. So uncanny is the wood duck
that he lets her pick him up. He lets her
nest him in the punk of a hollow log below
the hill. She looks into his dark eye and thinks
he just might be a wizard. a prophet.
What wisdom will his tidings bring?

Wonderment and lore, the shifting shape,
the spirit of things. Gaia sometimes thinks
she and her gifts have brought all of that
to heel — enchanted woodlands, runes
and stupors, fairy folk, wells
of the dead. That for her chartered ilk, the rules
won't miscarry. Yet when she
returns to his grotto, the prophet
is gone. And still she cannot say why
a stone rolls free of the moss. Or what
the mantis prays for. It's still a mystery to her
how the bee knows when to anoint
the bloom. A mystery
how wild onion chooses its green . . . .

Fences

The Habit of Shallow Breathing

I am not a scholar of deep breathing
— no practitioner of rugby or Puccini. How often does anyone
really breathe the full Möbius strip of a cat?
— that breath that guides your hand
from her pert nose and cheek and limbic knob
along and up and down the undulations of her back to tail's end
where with one slick
                flip, her circuit
lights your hand again from nose to cheek and to in-
finity. We laymen breathers, what we know to do with a deep breath
is spend it over candles on a cake, is help the medicine
go down without the benefit of sugar.
  I only clamp a deep breath on before the plunge
        into deep water.

            Shallow breathing
            settles in the day
       I first suspect that
       Mother lies. For all I know,
I too am guilty of something. Once
  I know what lives
        beneath the bed, my breath
  comes in links and wafers —
  in petal more than
bloom. Comes
without the room
  that wonder needs
  to arabesque into the next county.
Since then, shallow breathing comes
  like bits of dying,
        the step I think I hear
           in the shrubbery
           outside the window.

  But the habit of deep breathing serves more
than to birth our babies   *heh-heh-heh*
hoooo. In the check-out at the hardware store, your belly opens
like a lotus flower. When you doodle, break eggs in a bowl,

when you sort socks — deep breath brings
the center to your reaches.
Would that I could muster deep breaths daily — so that
even when the jury comes in with a verdict, I would hear
not my shallow breathing skitter but
— with only half a twist — boundaries giving way
and the long view purring.

All There Is To It

It helps if you have an old traffic cone
with the nib cut off; hang it in the open
upside down. Into this crush you'll slide
some of inspiration's cluck or fluster bottoms-up
where, with its head out the cone's
pointy end, it will settle
soon enough. But no matter
what you've heard from grandma
about an ax and two nails in a stump, do not
just pull the neck taut
and slice the head off — It's not very often
the first thing you think to write about
is all there is to it. You do
pull the neck taut, yes,
but as you close your hand over the head
there's the comb, meaty against the meat
of your palm. Feel feathers surrender and eyelids flutter
against the base of your thumb.
                                        Now
put the lexicon of your thumb to work,
that part they say makes the difference
between us and them. Figuratively speaking,
you've been practicing with this thumb
your whole life: how to button a shirt, how to
hammer a nail, how to reach an octave; how to
roll a joint, hull the strawberries, carry oils of sage and wintergreen
to your nostrils. How to soothe the satin edge
of a blanket. So let your thumb take its bearings
from the corrugations of the trachea
— let it perform its ancient rhymes. Roll
that thumb either side of the barrel of the windpipe
till it noses out the connotations of a pulse. That's where
you send the honed edge of your knife —
to the jugular but not to the airway. Because,
till your poem is flushed out,
you want the heart's blood to flow
without the heart stopping.

The Fear of Sleep

It's the slough of skin
that keeps you awake —
all that accumulates
and the cobwebs that form in the corners
when you're not looking.
Saliva pools in your throat
without the trigger of food
losing its way and
wanting to start over.
In your gut, fauna proliferate.
Hair and fingernails
split and fade.

If it were only the consequence
of not hearing the alarm
or of letting the coffee maker
bake dry, any jury of austere cats
might acquit you of falling
asleep. The priest
hearing such confession
might assign you 15,800 respirations a day
instead of the usual penance
counting sheep.

But coral can't help veining vessels
immersed in rest, nor can rust
resist to claim threads and joints
fallen still. Sandbags
levee against somnolence,
stemming the encroachment
of vine into lattice, of fear
into vitals. No slurry of volcanic ash
will overtake your thighs.

Every night the moon retreats from your bed
four one-thousandths of an inch:

If you fall asleep, what's to check
the return of tail and gills?
What's to keep gravity
from swapping temperaments with fire?

Dominion

You swam out of the cattails into the center
of the photo I was taking of my cat, who had joined
the dog and me on our stroll
    — and already you see how I am — *my* cat, *pfff,*
      as if —
my cat, who had joined us on our stroll out into the fields
past your slough. And there you were
in the center of the photo, as much
gift as handshake, muskrat arrowing
through the water right toward me
with that bit of bedding stuff in your mouth, engineering
ripples either side of you like
extravagant wings
— before landing at slough's edge to renovate
that tumble of rotting logs
into your lodge. This captured moment
was all I needed to think of you
as mine, and I showed you off
to friends with the wonder
of unearned trust. Didn't I.

    Leave it to the terrier: A later stroll
and at the tumble of logs at slough's edge a spree
seizes her, and she
    — imagine her shopping the jumble sales,
    drilling through the scatter of bras and cards of clip-on
    earrings, all grab and elbow —
till at some turn I miss, this spree of hers turns
savage, and this dog of mine
    — this dog who knows bed
    where I know bed —
she savages your den from the top
down till she all but disappears
inside, and then *quick-as-a-gasp* she
seizes you by the spine in such a savage
    — well, I —
    I have no words.

What's that old saying? If I love something, I should
let it go; and if it comes back

       — something.
       I don't remember.
       You might say twice I
let you go, and now your face
       — head of an arrow —
your face comes back and comes
again. It took my foot four tries
to override your broken fight and
toe you into a muck tub after the dog
carried you off. And when I carried you back
to the yard of your den at slough's edge
and tipped you out
       — Who doesn't want to die at home?
          — Is that more of the same? Am I
         still doing it? —
you thrust yourself forward half
a broken step and I
          — I carried the empty muck tub
back to my own yard, my dog,
my savage red and broken sanctimony.

Gaia, Mother Goddess of Life and the Bountiful Earth, Envies the Oral Tradition of Cows

Tonight again the cows' lowing and keening
keep Gaia from sleep — from her dreams
of betrayal and cunning. The plague
of their voices seeking their calves
calls to the very loam of her body; it aches
with their swollen udders.
When her right leg and thigh tingle,
when her ankle goes numb,
she knows her breasts — so much
in the practice of suckling young —
also will swell.

She leaves her bed and makes her way
onto the hillside above the feedlot
where the cows last saw
their calves. Where men
herded calves onto trucks.
A rabbit shrieks against night's
talons, but it's the epic voices of cows
that penetrate her like a brute
            mmuhh mmuhh mmuhh mmuhh
times dozens and more —

            The night breeze
stirs a lock of her hair
along the back of her neck,
and on her skin comes
a sweet, scorching froth seeping
into her bodice and shawl. The cows
bawl and shuffle. Tomorrow afternoon they'll resume
their bovine reserve, but tonight again
they have nowhere to go with their immortal
loss. Gaia holds her breasts close.
Envies the cows their clean break.

Cloven

Into the afternoon of the third day
she lies like half a round bale of hay
in the dirty snow of the feed lot.
Four cows face her like an unknown,
then shamble their rumps
to wind, having still that choice.
About the time I'm sure she's dead,
another cow steps at a considered pace
to where she lies to nudge
her ear. Does this cow take
or give with her long tongue? stroking,
stroking that ear with all she has
that is not cloven.

And then the ear's great head rises
and those two cows make their meaning.
The one shambles off. The other
watches her go.

Possum

Against the far wall of the shed,
this skulkfooted lurker recoils
behind pallets, angling for corners
I think are mine. In my vitals
digestion stops. With three .22 slugs
keen for their mark, I kneel,
one quiet finger staking my claim
to all I think I own. But when
the gun's moving parts balk,
belief backfires. My claim turns to lead
for want of a shot, and I retreat
through the hole in the wall
by which I came.

If She Had Grown Up to Be a Horse

as she had expected and planned those years
when she also got to name her baby brother for
Roy Rogers and when Teacher invited the class,
five at a time, to lunch on foot-long hot dogs
and cola, which her mother never gave her, and when
all of the small animals the class kept in cages
fed the big black-and-white cat over the weekend
after it got away from that frail little girl the one Friday
they had the show of pets from home and everybody thought
(hoped) it must have slunk out the door for home but instead
had hidden in a cupboard with the poster board
and white paste —
                    So if she had grown up to be a horse, certainly
first would have come to her the tail and mane, almost
the best reasons to *be* a horse instead of, say,
a princess, whose raiment could not be finer
than gold threads or pearls or one eagle feather
and so who would languish for want of movement
her body knew it knew of wind and rush and long hair
lapping her neck, fingering her shoulders, her flanks, and then
(and this *is* the best reason to grow up to be a horse) then would have come
swells of movement from inside her, seas and swells of her haunches' eager pull,
her shoulders' eager reach for the next bounding stride and the next
and the next, her hooves the willing servants of her rounding,
mounding back, gathering underneath her the high meadows and
the rocky outcrops — Till the playground, pinned down by
the school at one end and the ball diamond at the other,
rears up along the berm crowned by chain link
and pitches her down the range, propels her galloping
through herds of kids playing kickball and jacks in lumpish clusters
under their archless necks, their clatterless, drumless tennis shoes no match
for the music magic in her body — ready as she was, as she'd ever be,
for four legs instead of two.
                    She knew —
oh, she knew she was no, say, no princess; knew
she would not grow up to be queen. But never,
almost never in her long belief she would grow up to be a horse

37

did she believe she would ever plod,
did she expect a path that only laps back
on itself, nor did she plan the mill wheel,
the stone she makes to turn
over the stone that doesn't.

No Vacancy

Lila's mother laundered bed sheets maybe
once in spring and once in fall. So when, after
popcorn and toasted-cheese sandwiches,
you two girls giggled into that small bed,
you drew over yourselves the redolence
of warm bodies, the burr of rumpled laughter
and frayed wool sweaters with holes at the elbows.
    You nestled into a gamy, welcome
        welcome.

Your mother washed your sheets
once a week at least. That may be how
tonight and on the road, you know
more than you think you know. If I say,
    Someone's been sleeping in my bed,
it's not what you might think — not
some fair-haired fairy story and surely not
the smear you find on your own burgundy sheets
when your lover welcomes you home
from that all-girls' weekend in Detroit. In fact,

it's nothing you'll likely see — no
make-up smudge, no hair too long, too
dark. You might think soap, but it's nothing
bottled, dabbed or rinsed. As aroma, it's more
    the difference of his late rising
        and your early. The difference
        between a Chevy
    and a Ford. Between breathing
the russet feather from a red-tailed hawk, and then
        a wild turkey's bronze wing.
        There it is.

*

And so tonight, before you've barely
turned the cover down, how
something of these unfamiliar sheets rankles solitude
    and closes on your throat. Says
        Withdraw your hand. Says
No vacancy. Who lay in these sheets last
may know where those young girls went
but will not let you follow. May know why
you no longer forage in your dreams
but will not say. How tonight
    if I could say salt, you might think sweat.
    If I could say rust, you might think
        iron in the blood. And really

that may come as close to it as anything.

—Gospel hymn, lyrics by Civilla D. Martin

Wingbound I: Elegy on the Rose-Breasted Grosbeak Dead in Fencerow Scrub

Had you been the ubiquitous sparrow,
your struggle in the fork of two twigs
might have caught his righteous eye. He
might have sent someone to save you
while you still throbbed with consternation; sent
an angel — or me — to unhitch your wingpits from twiggy stocks
and return you to flight.   As it is, you sag
like a derelict ornament from your slender twig.
Compared to this rack by sapling, evisceration
by sharp-shinned hawk would have been grace. What good
can I do you now?

Did anything in the pattern of your exuberant flight
foretell this skirmish? in your liquid song
bode its strangulation? Once snagged,
you will have writhed and shuddered
till your head fell every way
wrong as a hoax. By the time our stars crossed,
the sun had baked your skin to bark, your eyes
to wafers, your wrenched and wretched shoulder blades
into a crucifixion. Perhaps you died for no reason
but that some god covets red.

In a shadow box shelved with photographs and books,
a plump bird carved from a single piece of wood and clipped to a peg
stretches up, his round eye steady. Come December,
maybe I'll clip it to a sprig of green and pretend
it's you: After all, intimacy has to bear
some shortcomings.
                              In the wind, your haggard plumage
still stirs. With the miracle of transfiguration,
you become a leaf.

Wingbound III: Elegy on A Barn Swallow, Trapped

She might have been destined for tea cups —
that sweep of cobalt glaze a-wing
on a translucent porcelain sky, where swallows
can and cannot fly, where they do

and do not jabber. Black pekoe and verbena
steaming in the curve of two hands
would have warmed her bird heart.

A different incarnation might have sent her
bedecked with gold into the afterlife
— amulets tucked against linen windings
and worthy of plunder, or with

the dry coracle of her own body
all the boat she would need
for ferrying up and down the river . . . .

How many migrations did her familiars make
in the time it took mites to strip this swallow's back
of its cobalt, to strip her wings to their spines
and lay the skin over her egg-reminiscent body

translucent and bare? A slow business,
and on-going, from the look of it. This naked,
desiccated hull, less weighty

than a breath, but veined with bones
and her many absent ardors: her slipstream, her up
flown from her interchangeable down; absent
her foliations of summer sunlight — and she, a spray

bred of an arrow and crazy eights —
How many migrations have her familiars made
in her lifetime of absences?

*

She's left here, really, almost nothing
but conjecture: A first flight, maybe two. Then
some rookie mistake. Now this pinched
and papery stillness longer than the linen strips that bind

an ancient corpse. I have robbed her accidental
tomb, absconded with what's left of her for my own
purposes: this jabber of words on paper, my

too much wonder   and imposition.
Hostess, priestess of the sill above my kitchen sink, she is
no less worthy of fine porcelain, of wrought gold,
in spite of the absence of it. As though either

would excite her ardors. As though porcelain, gold
or airy words were ever more than a swallow's flight —

Water Carries Her Offspring Full Term

The midwife moon
attends the bulge of tides,
and waves
contracting in the belly of the bayou
deliver the carcass of a deer
into the spring shore.
Where reeds break water,
beer cans and a rotting deck shoe
lap the newcomer laid wrong,
its neck wrung back on its unbelled throat.
Barely grazed incisors grin from bone,
and vertebrae lose their lock on hide;
their caps and vales
rake sunlight into strands.

From one season's womb a deer has drowned
by the slip of caul or grace.
Now water carries her offspring full term
to the regeneration of scavenger gulls.

Choir

Of Glue

I   Dead weight never means more
        than when the legs snap.
        A winch and chain drag the body of the gelding
        onto the renderer's truck
        where the fulcrum bulk of cattle
        and maybe another horse or two
        are more than his flightless bones can scale.
        The snap stops the last harmonic motion
        in those sprung legs, and gravity
        takes it last tug. Whatever
        his triumphs were, or none,
        he leaves in a rank cortege of flies,
        reckoned less than the price of meat.

        In the crucible of the rendering plant,
        resurrection stews. The fat boils out
        like the stone at the cave door rolling away.
        Everything but the nicker, they say,
        cooks down to fertilizer, food for dogs,
        till what remains is that infamous glue
        — a recipe old as hair.

II   If wood speaks in the tongues of angels,
        it's the glue that gives it voice —
        his everything and the nicker too.
        From August shade comes his marriage
        with spruce, maple, ebony — consummated
        in the seams of a violin, a double bass.
        From the wisdom of rosin,
        his own tail finds its rhythm and swing
        with the bow, its curve and recurve
        in the f-holes of the soundboard.
        He flexes his poll in the scroll and pegs
        for his love of trees. In the genius of glue
        he treads the meadows and plains again;
        he fills his lungs with the harmonics of wood.

*

The trout looks up and rises for the fly;
the lark ascends. And under the musician's hand
his hooffalls in spiccato amplify him,
amplify him!

Delirious Frogs Praise Their Vibrato Greens

The swamp road steams with frogs.
In the dark, asphalt recalls high sun
and simmers frogs to action.
The pavement is charged
with trill, its margins overrun
in the blind bliss of frogs.
Newly ripened, they buffet
the night's mulled vapors;
by hundreds, they effervesce,
celebrating their discovery of
      weight on legs,
        heat in their cold blood,
        the wonder of air —
and buoyed by the peals
of their own charmed voices.

When headlights scout the road,
frogs spark. The lamps mark
no end to them, but troll a pass
through their brassy clamor.
As the lights advance, frog ones
hush into hundreds,
and two sodden tracks unreel
tires' heavy way, grounding
      cold to asphalt,
      bliss to heat,
      frogs to steam —
so many ones back to rain.

But even as tail lights burn where
frog voices fade, more delirious frogs praise
their vibrato greens. Bead upon beaded note,
their one voice returns, a bubbling dome
that skirls up weightless
as those diminished ones
between their many toes. And that one voice
like tambourines and polished bells —

those many ones
      unfurl their long legs,
      toll their many throats,
      rally to be frogs —
claiming swamp and road, the night,
their many tributaries.

Following a successful heart transplant, Jennifer Sutton of
Hampshire, England, viewed her explanted organ in London during
the Wellcome Collection exhibit titled The Heart Explored.

In The Gallery of Her Chest, A Heart

In the gallery of her chest, a heart
worthy of installation learns his way around
the maelstrom of her blood
and falls in love with her bright chambers.
With his steady gait he woos her:
michaelmas daisies and orange peel,
the loyalty of friends,
and the masterpiece of her own hair
caught in a brush.

Did her excised heart shrug
— that wayward lover in its glass case —
feigning indifference at being found out?
Or was it her eye that throbbed between them
when they met again, her disbelief bound
by a tourniquet of memory and salutation?

No matter. Freed
from that dead heart's battering,
she reinvents herself like a widow.
She frames herself in trust and plans
for the holidays. And seeing her old heart now
for the worm'd boll it always was,
she takes her cue from the museum's
shuffling throng and turns, agreeing
they should go their separate ways.

When a Tree Falls in the Woods

Well before old poets failed to say
what never will be said,
cherry blossoms pledged their troth
to the two-trunk pine, and the sickle moon
rallied oceans. A younger sun
guided wheat. No hawk needed poets
to vanquish rabbits to cover, and
since ash first followed mud,
flowers have called the spruce's bluff —
poets or no. When sea and shore first
embraced, they learned each other's names
— and speak them still.

We might well want to hold
our tentative place — we for whom
old poets at last call and respond.
But it's bells, not poets,
who call the Whiteside girl over,
and some or other rock underground
that shifts and knocks on each coffin
to lead the neighbors to safety.

In the ceiling above our pillows,
a mouse with neither reason nor rhyme
taps out, "Do I make a sound?"

On "What the Old Poets Failed to Say," by Robert Bly

—with thanks also to Yehuda Amichai, Basho, Hafez,
John Crowe Ransom, and Thom Satterlee.

52

Fête de Mère, Ménilmontant, 1956

Under the blousey romance of peonies,
the boy in bare knees rollerskates home
to mother. Chivalry becomes him
easy as *l'esprit des fleurs* and the cut green stems
bound in his grubby fist by a few turns of string.

Abloom in the footwork of purpose, he veers
from playmates, the paring knife tucked in his sock
vouching for the full stride of his plan.
Bud to blossom, he's flush with mud
and the grace of love aforethought.

His flowers blush between her hands,
his own voice rippling their petals
when he greets her — not as the small boy's
Maman, but as his father does,
by her given name.

My Boy With Legs

I I don't think to count his legs
    in that first unswaddled tally: when
    fingers and toes tie ten to ten,
    and the delicate scrolls of each ear of two
    shape my hand with a mother's thanksgiving.

    As he toddles from diapers
    into piano lessons and little league,
    his steps multiply past notation, filling
    the staves of my life with melody,
    with chords. His hits, his errors,
    his runs batted in I'm sure
    I know by heart — all
    of his beats per measure.

II I've reckoned his birthdays on both hands
    by the time news sears the neighborhood:
    another mother's boy crosses the tracks
    in a crescendo of red flashing lights —
    Turning counter to plan, one bicycle wheel
    loses its bass line, loses its boy
    his romp for home, his count of legs.

    Imagination is a clot in the pulse of my infield,
    the coda that stops movement
    like a cramp. But even in arrest my heart
    takes inventory and posts a revised score.

III Blurred freckles in the sand lot
    like phrased quarter notes
    make of my heart a cornet.
    My boy steals third on his two legs,
    and reveille sounds another day of gratitude.

    That's my boy there, on a wonder of legs—
    Two legs, and counting.

—With thanks to PJH

Think It the Pleasantest Thing

If you find yourself in a chair swing
made of planks and pushed from behind
    by a nine-year-old boy in the doldrums between
    the end of summer and the beginning of school —

    try to forget about sirens rising and falling
in their approach through the hills of your stomach
    — in that nausea of what's already urgent and only likely
        to get worse —

Try to remember your mother's percale sheets
wind-billowing from her clothesline; her
    diaphanous curtains breathing at an open
        window. Resist imagining your head

    malformed between concrete blocks or under
the dead weight of a rodeo bull leaning on his own
    skull. It's opportunity missed even pinching the skin
        over the bridge of your nose or drilling

    your fingers under your hair clear to your medulla
oblongata. Imagine instead the amber waves of bourbon
    swirled in a glass, the banked curve of a skirt hem swiveling
        from hips. Let your movement

    hypnotize the leaves on the nearby lilac
like a cobra weaving before a mouse — then swallow
    the sun feet first and let your own peristalsis work it back
        through your vestibules to your open mouth

    and again up to the bottoms of your feet. Be yourself
the hands and the measure of butcher's twine
    that become Cat's Cradle, with their shared swoop
    and gather. Be the hammock the cradle

*

the echo the womb. And when the boy drifts away
into his own equilibrium, become the whistle
           spun 'round his finger by its chain
           and slid freefall into his pocket.

With Apologies to the Goldfinch

What's not to love? this perfect day
to dig bull thistle — ragged and meddlesome
along the paddock fence. Though
the garden fork's tang is so loose in the shaft
you have to work the fork head out of the soil
by hand, the soil itself is moist, the sky
mottled, the wind eager against two layers
of shirt. You welcome the good company of cats
held to their bellies by chittering
barn swallows. The fork coaxes the soil
loose around the roots, and you massage
the thistle's formidable spines
down against your gloved palm
before you true your feet and shoulders,
pelvis and quads
                to pull.

                            So what's not
to love? For muscle, it's work; for roots
the earth. Swallows love sky, and sky,
wind. Cats love a bit of ruckus —
which they can then ignore. Even the tang
— dare I say it? — loves the shaft, evidence
notwithstanding.

        By lunchtime a ragged meddle of bull thistle
fills the wheelbarrow twice over. For love of seed,
the goldfinch takes his perfect flight
elsewhere, to hedges and woods edge
where blooming thistle still stands.
                      And you — you
tip the wheelbarrow's load onto the fire pit
then work some ease back into your shoulders
with a roll, welcoming into your lungs
the tang of wind and sky.

Somewhere in the pasture, the dog
noses into the nests of red-winged blackbirds
to inhale their musk.

Rain Hazes Earthworms in Divots
That Horses Leave Behind

Worms raise hosannas
to acreage — honoring
slough and rot
with their five hearts
and working dirt cheap.
Disciples of both air
and water,
they genuflect their way
through the valleys
of shadows of clay,
mouths full of communion
and trash talk.

But when rain falls
too full of itself,
it shrugs off worms' reputation
as reconcilers
of apples to oranges.
Waters rise, and
soil's fraternal handshake
goes limp.
Worm hydraulics fail.

No longer good at math,
tinkerers with wood,
lovers of music,
worms wave
as if from floating rooftops
for a helping hand
out. How long can they hold
a primitive breath?
They might as well
be bait.

*

Rain will love worms
to death
unless a child hears
their soggy voices
and wades in to carry them
to deep grass on high ground.
Let some poet try
rhyming *worm*
with *muse* — try
with just her one heart
overturning an acre of ground
in metaphors for chewing dirt.

Roadkill

Bloated raccoons
grimace where their wits martyred them,
      at the side of the road where their grip
         on the tree of life relaxed mid-shinny.

Around the shoulders of a weedy cross,
    a sun-bleached plastic wreath
        like the slung arm of a drunk — A name
in paint slurred by weather and winter's road salt —

    Where the road Ts,
        a car turns neither left nor right, but
bumpers-over-the-grille into the ditch.
    At the intersection where a stop sign
        should have been priest enough — Along
the stretch of highway where some driver expects
        not one revelation —

Is this guidepost where shades of the dead come
seeking the comforts of a worn teddy bear or
snapshots like visions of saints and virgins in zip-lock bags?
Is this scaffold where they pawn
the tennis racket and the American flags
so they can return one day to claim their faded effects?

On the verge, the six teats of a possum
      balloon from her marsupial pouch,
        her young the size of peanuts
riding nipples and rot gas up, crisp witness
      to the steel-belted rumble of long-distance haulers
        and garbage trucks.

Who bothers to make pilgrimage to these shrines? Doe
      whose fawn straddles the double-yellow line
      to steep in miraculous cures? Squirrel, who,
      from his own skidmark, raises the lit candle of his tail?
      Goldfinch, who leaves the yellow feather that says,
        "I, too, was here."

Keystone

After more than a year of pestilence
and suspicion, we convene. We approach
the backyard fire pit, we friends of friends, hoisting
web folding chairs and shy behind cloth masks,
knees and elbows cautious of proximity.

But once our paper plates fill with burger
and fruit salad, we peel our masks away
and reintroduce ourselves to the full complement
of a face: to dimples. to hook noses, ski-slope
and button — nostrils flaring and nostrils
pinched. to the pimple, the pout, the tongue tip,
the scowl, the wince. to lips drawn tight over teeth
and lips drawn easy. to the O of surprise — a mustache? —
and the O of *b'lieve I will*. to an incisor slightly
askew, enamel stained by coffee, the dazzle
of a gold cap. to that one bicuspid.   missing.

A man whose face I've never seen
greets colleagues with a round of handshakes
like he's been saving up. I too rise. Eye to eye and
hand to hand, in turn we say our names. His name — his
face — I don't recall.
                    But his hand I'd know
again: Bone and meat, dry and strapping.
         A haul up out of the ditch.
    The keystone of a stone archway.

*At the Impressionist Exhibition of 1881, the public and most
art critics found Gauguin's* Étude de Nu (Suzanne Sewing)
homely and vulgar.

My Body, This Aging Cheese

My body, this aging cheese,
affronts them like a mold, as though
beneath my burred rind
I were not still another woman's
cream-skinned daughter, tending
to her torn petticoat.
                 This curdled lap,
these clotted breasts slough
their *tut*s and rancid glances.
If our intent had been a pose, I'd have
sat this unmade bed like a throne.

Instead, I ripen and mend. And if
they miss the grace even I can see
of thimble needling thread from one stitch
to the next, they miss, too,
that flavor's in the fat, and that,
in full time, like sin
generations removed from the original,
they will lick me all over for the salt.

Deus In Machina

The muse of that old Ford truck
answered every time,
scattering hay chaff up the defrost
like inspiration. Though under a load
internal rhyme in the manifold
threatened its oral tradition with rupture
or infarct, it still made
boisterous and stiff-shocked
consonance with the road and
meant something. Sheet metal improvised a floor
over the churning refrain of the underworks
but left the stalk of the accelerator,
worn smooth, with a collar of daylight to welcome
rust. One stomp or two from my boot threw
the slant rhyme of brights
into the unstressed feet of night.
A turn on vise grips coaxed
scansion from the wipers,
the meter in their dry arcs scoring glass.

Whether over pavement or rutted fields,
the dog drafted winter haiku from air leaks
at broken window seals, her nose
quilling calligraphy on the pane.
And while the epic clutch pedal
composed my thigh in a hero's workout,
the gear shift wanted my hand
light, my wrist loose
— a caesura in a braille sonnet —
that old Ford muse ever
twittering like a fan belt.

Sanctuary

Two Men Selling Honey
Consider the Woman With Pears

They brought honey to sell,
two men. In a market stall they set up
a folding table with oil cloth
from the trunk of their car.
No farm sign, no power cords —
just an umbrella for shade,
a tackle box of change
and crates of honey in jars.
Not bad for a summer of bees' work.

Each brought a Thermos of coffee
it looked like, and a couple of
web-frayed chairs. As the plump
sun warmed and hummed its way
above garden shoulders, above roof lines,
the jars amused them in balanced skeps,
in amber prisms. The coffee, too,
amused them, or seemed to.
With each jar they sold, they cross-
pollinated a few half-lies —
probably doing no one much harm —
then settled into the give of their chairs,
passing the thermos back and forth
while jars of honey rearranged themselves.
The hours performed their patterned dance,
and the sun through glass cells
cast pollen flares on the oil cloth,
refracted petals twirling slow.

Once they opened the second thermos
they found themselves watching
the woman with pears.
Not young. More their own age,
they thought. They watched mostly her hands,
or pears, or pears in hand. . . .
As she settled each pear in a basket

— quart, peck, half-peck —
the bulb of the fruit, its yellow curve
and weight, nested in the bulb of her palm,
an intimate safety, its neck narrowing
in the small swell of rapport with her fingers.
Even from where they sat they could see
she knew her fruit by heart, without bruises.
One paper sack after another left her
— gravid with pears
blessed by her ripe hand.

Without ever speaking of it
— or her, or them —
each lost himself a few moments of time
envying ripe fruit,
never once counting the money,
but tasting the sweetness
on his own tongue.

Lost and Found

In the house now burn fewer lights — one
near the window where nights she sits
with her knitting, soothing
as lanolin. She can't even guess — socks?
A cap. Or scarf? A tea cozy?
The knitted folds that shawl her lap
spill either side of her knees, a pool
of loops intersecting loops. Stitches —
Who's counting?

In a fairy tale, she might tell unfinished stories
for a thousand and one nights, might
grow her hair long as a tower
is tall. (A receiving blanket?
An afghan for the day bed maybe.) She would ride
on the backs of beavers needling upstream
to knit themselves a hearth from whatever's
at hand. She would become the beaver.

Her shrewd hands assume the wit
to stem a breach at the sound of water
seeping. Over long weeks,
her light burns, and waves of knitted folds
pond the floor. The day she finally looks up,
it's not a cap or sweater spread before her,
but a lodge cozy. An acreage. A wide, still water.

Wingbound II: Elegy Shy of Lamentation

For now, in this deep winter, wind.
No scab, no scale, no worry of codling moth

stirs the orchard. Only wind.   Elsewhere,
up-risers storm the streets. Jetsam bobs

in the current, trailing poisons, trailing
spores. The earth moves, the sea

opens up, and what was higher
becomes lower; what had been low

rises.   Here, it's wind that disquiets kilter.
Even rabbits cannot make tracks across deep snow

for nights on end.
                  In an apple tree

the great horned owl closes yellow eyes
and freezes to the branch. He dies

from the outside in — mark of both chance
and covenant. Later, a boy will find him there.

For now, light banks off the white feathered bib
under the great shrine of his head,

trailing his claim to night, trailing moon.

Buffalo Plaid

Beyond the latitude and longitude
of your own checked shirt, your compass
teetered and spun. From tree stand

or blind, as though your life depended on it,
you could take down any turkey or buck
where it fled, wasting no shot. But

navigating that timber and brush, you spiraled
through camouflage browns:
beech, oak, moss, rye —

lager, ale, single malt. All
you could find slurred in leaf mold
was your own spoor, as if

you trod with one foot staked,
scuffing out your own footprints
in revolutions no wider than your jacket.

Even with our signal pyres blazing
you would not find your way back. You
were bound to break camp without bearings,

your thumb releasing the safety,
and trusting only your one finger
to point you the way out.

So many days we groped through shambles
toward the steady curve of the horizon,
reclaiming the best of you —

your jeans and shirts to flannel the bed
with the comfort of handwork; your face
quilting ours, and the refrigerator door —

*

We make our way still
on the red and black grid of your buffalo plaid.
With your good eye, we triangulate

sense with memory and arm ourselves
in the scent of you, stalking
your unbound heat.

Foreclosure

I.   The sun studies the far wall
from the kitchen window. Already he has forgotten
the blocky real estate of the refrigerator
for the copper tubing that remains,
the electrical outlet with its rag of cobweb
but no plug, no hum. He brushes past
where the cat saved up kibble and other bounty
under the absent stove: two keys,
one book of stamps, the checkbook register,
a hearing aid, and four unopened clips
of candy Pez — all
now alight in the empty room,
as though, in passing,
his hip has dialed up the flame.

II.   Make Offer:
Baskets, jig-saw puzzles and board games,
place-mats, table cloth with matching napkins.
Two potted philodendron, baskets,
clothes hangers bundled with masking tape, children's books
from ducklings to dinosaurs, *National Geographic*,
Reader's Digest, Bubble Wrap, baskets. Plastic shovel
and pail. Pedal car. Tea pot shaped like English cottage.
Tea pot shaped like pineapple.
Baskets.
Free.

III.   Screwed to the door frame
a clipboard the size of a post card
where drop-ins left notes: *Sorry*
we missed you — we
owe you lunch! Will stop back
later. D & S. The pencil hangs
from a knotted string, lead broken,
its eraser dry as a nut.

IV.   On the open porch, an indifferent breeze
nudges the slatted swing on its way through.

Matching blue shutters and window boxes
hang on while they can, but the swing — ahh.
Hoofclops from an Amish buggy passing
rap against clapboard, their knock unanswered
by a terry cloth robe and Sunday morning paper,
a cigarette at dusk.

V.   Jostled into a cardboard box,
iris dug from along the walk as some kind of remedy
cannot find their list of things to do.
First the root, and then the rain.
Still in the box at the corner of the garage,
they give up trying to become an Easter hat.

VI.   The bad news: Limbfall from old maples
spindles sod with a shrug after the good fight.
The good news: Limbfall welcomes sun
to grass. Too much of a good thing,
maybe: Grass claims the collateral in
wood's exposed grain. Grass claims cracks
in asphalt, claims raspberry canes,
claims compost pile, fire pit, Adirondack chair;
grass claims lawn, and goes to seed.

VII.   The neighbor's drive seems twice as long
with nowhere to carry gossip
from the post office. Overdue news
backs up and cools. Fix-it hands
find their place repossessed.

VIII.   The sun curls into the corner by the back door
like the dog they tried to give away
who would not dun them for what it cost her
navigating the road's shoulder
back to this stoop. And if no one lets her in today,
perhaps tomorrow.
Or the day after.

Father, As Though Sealing You In

When even agonal respirations
cease to prick your lungs
and I have only just faded in reflection
from the apples of your eyes,
it seems more than courtesy
to close your cooling lids
against small white larvae that might
chew their way in. In old films
a wand of hand passes over
those dateless coins, and, *presto
change-o*, they blanch into two closed eyes
settled in the spent purse of a face.
But mine is no magician's hand: when
I pass my hand down your face,
your eyes do not close.

Not so my reflection should waver again
in those dim coins but so
an ease like still life with fruit
should answer the spell I cast —
this is why I call down the glow
from the candle my steady hand
would conjure. My fingertips
press your eyelids shut
to smother any grub of doubt — mine
or yours — as though sealing you in
behind the skin of your death
would spare us our loss of each other,
and that loss the temptation
to worm its way back out.

Orbit

Hooves tread
the precipice
at the edge
of his flat earth.
Where his other eye
used to be,
a tympanum of skin
spans bone.
It is not the rope
or bit that frees him,
no: his muzzle
reads the earth as globe
in the orbit
of her cupped hand.

—for MB and Syncopation

If Mouse Could Slip Her Skin

If Mouse could slip her skin
the way a snake does, she could leave
the felt glove of herself
snagged from the slip-hinge of his jaw

and skedaddle. Alas, it is not
so, and when the snake flicks his tongue
for her heat, she must choose: flee
or freeze, heart dizzy either way.

Yet what way is fear to live?
Mouse crafts her nest up under the tarp
with feathers and grass,
with filaments of milkweed

sails. And by her own cheeks
she smuggles in the sloughed skin
of the snake, wends his cold and bloodless
discard into a feathery boa to wreathe her litter

— to snug her young and welcome them.

Swimming with Fishes

—Pantoum after Zandomeneghi's
In Bed, *1878*

A sea turtle swims in the girl's repose,
weightless under waves

of eiderdown, rumpling the light.
From the wallpaper next to her bed,

weightless under waves
of even reptilian beats,

the wallpaper next to her bed
blooms — frond and undulation.

Even, reptilian beats
mingle the hair over her pillow,

and bloom — frond and undulation —
with kelp and jellyfish. Petals

mingle with the hair over her pillow.
Shrimp tempt her prehistoric beak

among kelp and jellyfish. Petals
scatter as she passes —

shrimp tempting her prehistoric beak,
sea turtles swimming in the girl's repose

and scattering as she passes —
eiderdown rumpling the light.

How Easily Does the Eavestrough

How easily does the eavestrough
disown the logic
to divert the rain away
from a foundation —
seamless slick
aluminum runs
in one of forty colors.
How easily does the gutter
recall the furrow.

Birch catkins
drop and roll.
Seeds of the maple
wing in; willow
flotsam, beetle jetsam
caudle
through the dark season
below the roof's valley
next to the chimney,
where the climate
of a shady copse
kneels. Ancient cunning
still works in the brew.

If I were not posted to this ladder,
I too would kneel
over hands pious
with burgundy humus,
raise it to my face,
smell it, kiss it
for the rudiments
that in the furrow
tease the germ to unfurl.

But rain will come again;
so too logic.
How easily does the rain
recall the river.

The Novelty of Heat

I A bovine heat loafs
   on the stubble of July,
   pants stale humidity
   and masticates days
   to a wad.

   Towels won't dry.
   Salt won't shake.
   Matches won't exert themselves
   enough to catch.
   Swelter smears any breath on skin,
   and the only eye that doesn't squint
   is black-eyed Susan's by the fence
   — and it droops.

   Morose robins sag over a branch,
   their beaks slack, their wing hollows
   airing. Heavy as laying hens,
   doves on the wire
   mourn their loss of lift.

   A listless dusk rolls over and
   yawns between horizons.
   In the dark next to the attic
   heat seals my flesh and bones under a lid
   to the dead weight of the mattress.
      I wish I could levitate to sleep.
      I wish I could sleep.

II When a cooling front skips overland
   she kushes heat along.
   Full of industry, she plucks
   the sheet off the floor
   and unplugs the fan. All night
   she herds dust bunnies along baseboards.
   She eddies rose petals from spent blooms.
   At dawn, she coddles my arms in long sleeves,
   sweetening the tang of chill on bare legs.

*

The furnace clears its throat,
warning against her fresh airs.
She's unrepentant, as am I —
we leave the windows open, all and wide,
and the furnace surrenders to work.
I stand on the register in each room,
the steam from a mug of tea heavy
with cream nuzzling my eyelids and lips,
and the tease of forced air fluttering
the short hems at my thighs.
        My body sways to the rhythm of warmth.
        I flirt with the novelty of heat.

Labyrinth

Five times I paint the same image,
with variations: a horse
granting asylum to a boy.

You wear the clothes of a much larger man, clothes
that get larger by the day. By the hour.

The hay arrives — late for second cutting
but sweet and deeply, deeply green.

Across town, a man much older than you
sits with his book and two cats — his neck and shoulders
draped in a wrap his niece has made.

In the morning, five deer break from shelter
in the slough. Their white tails startle
the shorn soybean field.

A neighbor comes unbidden and unannounced
with a shovel and a sack of Quikrete
to reset the listing mail-box post.

You sit on a chair in the shower and let
the water run over you.

Starlings gather in the cottonwood, their brassy
Hitchcock chatter belying your vulnerability.
And your grace.

A woman dark inside her fringed hood
walks four big dogs and pushes
an aging Airedale in a stroller.

Before clearing out your refrigerator,
I stand in the shower and let
the water run over me.

The brick mason on his padded knees
celebrates the circumference of the labyrinth.
And its center.

*

We wheel you out to the end of the jetty, where
you throw a key into the ocean.

From the pillow, your voice rises
with intonations of some totem animal. We can tell
you're singing — and join in.

In the belly of a pile of grass clippings and leaves,
compost begins to breathe.

The Hands of Amish Boys

Amish boys grow from their hands in.
Their hands answer the call to manhood
well before their beards do, before their bowlcut heads
grow into their straw hats. Big as Bibles,
the hands of Amish boys dwarf
their own arms, and their dinner forks;
it's a two-fisted meal that fuels such hands.

In those hands' most holy moments,
orphan lambs suck fingers, and fingers
cup the chins of calves to stroke their palates.
The hands of Amish boys lead those stubbly snouts
into buckets of warm milk,
then ease their knuckles out, mid suck.

When light idles, the hands of Amish boys
shun mischief. They root into the dark cellar
of trouser pockets up to their wrists
till prodigal work returns. Pockets quiet
the melee in those hands.

Then, with inspired bone, boys leverage salvation
with hands like crafted tools, nicked and worn
and grooved spans — those hands ready
to punch leather and hew wood for the stove,
to shake on their deal with God — even when they still stand
in the shade of their fathers' hat brims
and the haunches of big horses.

Acknowledgments

I'm pleased to recognize the following publications where these poems first appeared.

Atticus Review - With Apologies to the Goldfinch
The Aurorean - Orbit
Big Scream - Cloven; Father, As Though Sealing You In;
    Roadkill; When A Tree Falls in the Woods
Blue Mountain Review - Swimming With Fishes
The Briar Cliff Review - The Kissing Post; Lost and Found
    (published as "Losing the Count"); The Novelty of Heat
Calliope - *Deus In Machina*
Cape Rock - All There Is To It
Controlled Burn - How Easily Does the Eavestrough; Two Men
    Selling Honey Consider the Woman With Pears
Cottonwood - Wingbound III: Elegy on a Barn Swallow, Trapped
Cream City Review - The Hands of Amish Boys
Dogwood - There Is Room in a Horse for the Whole Boy
    (published as "Asylum")
Driftwood - Water Carries Her Offspring Full Term
Dunes Review - In the Gallery of her Chest, A Heart
Iconoclast - Possum
Jet Fuel Review - No Vacancy; Think It the Pleasantest Thing
Literary Life - Wingbound IV: *Dénouement* (1st place tie)
The MacGuffin - My Body This Aging Cheese (1st place: 16th
    National Poet Hunt)
Nimrod International Journal - Argiope, Goddess of Small
    Repute
Ninth Letter - Dominion
North Dakota Quarterly - If Mouse Could Slip Her Skin
Parting Gifts - The Fear of Sleep; My Boy With Legs
Peninsula Poets - Buffalo Plaid (Poetry Society of Michigan
    category "Loss" winner 2010); Wingbound II: Elegy Shy of
    Lamentation (Poetry Society of Michigan category "Nature"
    winner 2021)
Poet Lore - Foreclosure
*Song of the Owashtanong: Grand Rapids Poetry in the 21st
    Century*. David Cope, ed. - Rain Hazes Earthworms in
    Divots that Horses Leave Behind
South Carolina Review - If She Had Grown Up to Be A Horse
Spoon River Poetry Review - Of Glue

Talking River Review - Carry Me; Delirious Frogs Praise Their
Vibrato Greens; *Fête de Mère*; Touch My Face; Gaia, Mother
Goddess of Life and the Bountiful Earth, Consecrates the Bones;
Gaia, Mother Goddess of Life and the Bountiful Earth, Envies
the Oral Tradition of Cows
Third Wednesday - Wingbound I: Elegy on the Rose-Breasted
Grosbeak Dead in Fencerow Scrub
Twyckenham Notes - Give a Man a Fish; Labyrinth
3288 Review - Navigating Toward the Foothills of November

These poems have also benefited from the insights and
encouragement of Joy Gaines-Friedler, Philip Jung, Katie Kalisz, GF
Korreck, Walter Lockwood, Lawrence Manglitz, Rodney Torreson,
Kimberly Wyngarden, and, kindest of advisors, Jack Ridl.

Many thanks as well to Christine Stephens-Krieger and Scott Krieger
for their considerable labors and generosity of spirit in making this
collection a reality.

Author Bio

Barbara Saunier grew up in West Michigan, and wrote her first poem at the age of six — which she then gave to the family dentist, who kept it in her file until he retired. She took up writing poetry again several decades later, along the way supporting herself operating a solder pot on an assembly line, decorating furniture, life modeling, and free-lance writing — eventually picking up degrees from the University of Michigan and Western Michigan University. Her work has been published in many journals and reviews; it was also honored with first place in *The MacGuffin* 16th National Poet Hunt and in several other local and regional competitions. After teaching at Grand Rapids Community College for twenty-seven years, she is now retired — from teaching, from farm life, from horses and riding dressage. But she still drives a stick shift and does not color her hair.

www.ingramcontent.com/pod-product-compliance
Lightning Source LLC
Chambersburg PA
CBHW051328120626
46547CB00015B/2449